Forex

A Beginner's Guide to Currency Trading

MICHELLE MICHAELS

Copyright © 2016 Michelle Michaels

All rights reserved.

ISBN-13:

978-1535225618

ISBN-10:

1535225610

DISCLAIMER

This book is designed to provide information that the author believes to be accurate on the subject matter it covers, but it is sold with the understanding that neither the author nor the publisher is offering individualized advice tailored to any specific portfolio or to any individual's particular needs, or rendering investment advice or other professional services such as legal accounting advice. Professional services should be sought if one needs expert assistance in areas that include investment, legal, and accounting advice. There is a substantial risk of loss associated with trading these markets. Losses can and will occur. No system or methodology has ever been developed that can guarantee profits or ensure freedom from losses. No representation or implication is being made that using this information will generate profits or ensure freedom from losses. The trade examples provided were hypothetical only and were prepared with the benefit of hindsight. No hypothetical trading record can completely account for the impact of financial risk in actual live trading. Additionally, this book is not intended to serve as the basis for any financial decisions, as a recommendation of a specific trading system. Your personal financial circumstances must be considered carefully before investing or spending money. No warranty is made with respect to the accuracy or completeness of the information contained herein, and both the author and the publisher specifically disclaim any responsibility for any liability, loss or risk, personal or otherwise, which is incurred as a consequence, directly or indirectly, of the use and application of any of the contents of this book.

CONTENTS

1	What is Forex?	Pg 6
2	The Basic Concepts of the Forex Market	Pg 11
3	Forex Market Hours and Time Frames	Pg 20
4	Three Major Types of Market Analysis	Pg 26
5	Choosing the Right Broker	Pg 36
6	The Truth About Successful Forex Trading	Pg 41
7	Two Simple Robust Trading Strategies	Pg 46
8	Conclusion & EA Offer	Pg 53
9	Recommended Resources	Pg 55

1

What is Forex?

The Foreign Exchange market commonly known as Forex is the place where we can trade one country's currency against another country's currency and unlike stocks these financial instruments are traded in pairs. For instance, we all know that the currency of the USA is the US Dollar and the currency of the United Kingdom is the Great British Pound, which would be shown as GBP/USD. This market provides the unique opportunity to buy the US Dollar by selling the Great British Pound, and vice versa.

The market is not limited to this pair only, rather many different currency pairs are being traded in the Forex market, including all of the world's major currencies, 2nd tier and exotic currencies which will be discussed a little later. A Forex trader can buy or sell any currency pair at any moment without concerns for the economic situation thus Traders have the unique opportunity of making a profit by buying the high yielding currency and/or selling the low-yielding currency. It is immaterial that the currency must do well to make the profit from this market given they are traded in pairs. No matter how well or bad a currency is doing, you will still have an opportunity to make a profit out of it. It sounds a little confusing at first, but it is quite simple really.

Advantages of Trading the Forex Market

The rising popularity of the Forex market remains closely associated with its high liquidity, leverage and low cost of entry. In the past, trading Forex was limited to larger institutions and banks. Thanks to advanced technologies and market progression, retail traders can now play in the Forex sandpit with any amount of startup capital and, from the comfort of their own home. All one needs to do is signup and complete a simple identity verification process with the online Broker of choice.

You can even start Forex trading by creating a demonstration account with any broker without spending any of your own money. A demonstration account, or what is commonly referred to as a demo account, is basically a simulation account that has the same features as a live account, however you are not putting any of your own funds at risk. It is a great tool to help you develop trading systems and also familiarize yourself with the features of your broker's trading platform.

In the introduction, I already touched on the daily volume traded amount of around $5.5 trillion, which makes it near impossible to manipulate the market. This market is 25 times larger than the New York stock market (NY stock market is the largest Stock Market in the world). The Forex market is open 24hrs 5 days a week. Traders from all around the world participate in this huge financial market in three major sessions. These are the Asian Session, the European Session and the US Sessions. This wide range of trading time offers the Trader the opportunity to trade the Forex market at a time convenient to them without interfering with their daily activities.

Successfully trading Forex and making a living from it requires knowledge about how it all works along with strict discipline. This next section will familiarize you with the very basic concepts of Forex trading that you will require for trading the financial market, as it is of utmost importance that your foundation is solid before you start your journey to become a full-time trader.

The potential for financial freedom via the Forex market is right at your computer.

How is Profit Made in the Forex Market?

The currency value of each country is continuously changing. The change in the monetary value of any currency depends on the country's economy and other financial related factors. You often see in the newspaper or online, that the US Dollar is broadly stronger against the British Pound and vice versa. So with so much movement in a country's currency, you will see plenty of movement in prices on most pairs, most of the time. This is especially true around major news, for example, when a country is setting its Interest Rates or releases its Employment Figures etc.

If the value of Euro is trending up relative to USD then you can buy the Euro and make a good amount of profit by selling it when the price is much higher. Let's give an example using the EUR/USD pair. Suppose you have bought 100 EURO with 120 USD thinking that its value will go much higher in the near future. Over the next couple of week the value of EURO skyrockets! Now you have decided that you want to sell your EUROs. So when you go to the market and sell the 100 EURO, you receive 140 USD, which is a $20 profit

What Do We Trade in Forex?

Forex trading doesn't require the physical involvement of buying and selling commodities. Simply, money is traded in the Forex market. We trade one country's currency against another country's currency. It is similar to buying or selling shares in a company.

For example, when we buy the Japanese Yen we are actually buying the share of the Japanese economy. We hope that the Japanese economy is doing well against its major rival so that we can make the profit by selling the Yen in the market sometime in the future at a higher price. Traders use different techniques like technical analysis and fundamental analysis in order to gauge the strength of a currency pair in the Forex market.

In general, the currency exchange rate is the direct reflection of one country's economy compared to another country. Now we all know what exactly is traded on the Forex market, let's look at the eight major currencies traded across the world.

Major Currencies Traded in the World

Country	Currency	Symbol	Nickname
United States	Dollar	USD	Greenback
Euro zone members	Euro	EUR	Euro
Japan	Yen	JPY	Yen
Great Britain	British Pound	GBP	Cable
Switzerland	Swiss Franc	CHF	Swissy
Canada	Dollar	CAD	Loonie
Australia	Dollar	AUD	Aussie
New Zealand	Dollar	NZD	Kiwi

Basically, the currency symbol consists of three letters. The first two letters of the symbol represent the country's name and the last letter represents the country's currency. For instance, the first two letters of the symbol USD represents the country name (United States) and the last letter represents the currency name.

These 8 currencies are called the major currencies in the Forex market because they represent the majority of all Forex transactions conducted by the major players in this market.

The Majors are traded in the following pairs, notice they are all relative to the value of the US Dollar.

The Majors

EUR/USD	The Euro and the US Dollar
USD/JPY	The US Dollar and the Japanese Yen
GBP/USD	The British Pound and the US Dollar
USD/CHF	The US dollar and the Swiss Franc

Then we have the Minor Currencies also referred to as "Minors". The Minors consist of all other currency pairs and cross currencies.

The Minors

EUR/AUD	Euro and the Australian Dollar
GBP/JPY	British Pound and the Japanese Yen
EUR/CHF	Euro and the Swiss Franc
USD/NZD	US Dollar and the New Zealand Dollar
AUD/JPY	Australian Dollar and the Japanese Yen
GBP/CHF	British Pound and the Swiss Frank

There are various other currencies traded, however to a much smaller extent. Some examples of these would be the South African Rand, the Mexican Peso, the Turkish Lira, and the Singapore Dollar etc.

2

The Basic Concepts of the Forex Market

Every time you travel to another country, knowingly or unknowingly, you are actively participating in the foreign exchange market. The moment you exchange your own country's currency with the other country's, is the very moment you become a part of this huge financial market. The concept of trading the currency pairs is very simple even though the Forex market has extensive applications in the real life economy.

Previously, I talked about the eight major currencies in the world. Forex traders take advantage of the fluctuations of interest rates and exchange rates of countries. The market is constantly moving up and down due to the continuous release of major economic news and other relevant financial events affecting each individual country. A successful Forex Trader is aware of these economic news events and will use this information to assist with trading decisions. An overseas traveler may do the same, where they may exchange their home currency for another well before their departure date as they believe a certain event may affect one or the other currency. The traveler is after the best exchange rate so they get more 'bang for their buck' so to speak in the country they are visiting.

The Forex market is seen by some as way more advanced than the stock market in terms of returns, flexibility and reliability. Traders trade the currency which directly reflects the economy of a country. This market can rarely be manipulated as the currency value depends on many international and national factors, which are very difficult to alter. A trader who has a sound knowledge about the eight major pairs in the Forex market, and the fundamentals that may affect them, has a distinct advantage over those traders that don't.

How Does a Forex Trade Work?

Forex trading is a combination of buying and selling the currency of two different economies at the same time. For example, if the GBP/USD in the Forex market is quoted as 1.4500, it simply represents that 1.4500 USD is required to buy 1 GBP. Every single currency pair is subject to the same rule, where you are simultaneously buying one currency and selling another currency.

If you hold a trade open overnight, then your Broker may either pay you interest on that transaction, or you may have to pay interest on that transaction. This is sometimes referred to as the 'carry' or the 'swap'. This is determined by the currencies country of origins' official Interest Rate.

Let's assume that the interest rate of JPY is 0.5% and that of New Zealand is 4%. So, when a trader buys the NZD/JPY pair, he or she can expect to earn an annualized 4% interest rate of return on the NZD, but have to pay an annualized rate of 0.5% based on the fact that they sold the JPY. So by buying the NZD/JPY, the trader will earn a nett profit of 3.5%. But if the trader sold the NZD/JPY pair, then the same interest rates apply, so the trader would be charged 3.5%.

This is something a trader has to be aware of during times of high interest rates and also if they want to hold open trades for an extended period of time. There are traders that seek out these Carry trades, taking advantage of the interest paid to them, where they deliberately look for high yielding pairs to trade and hold them long term based on careful analysis, where even if they suffer a small loss on the actual trade itself, they may make more than enough from the total interest received to end up profitable in the long run. It's not that easy to do in times of very low interest rates though.

Effect of Leverage Over Returns

High leverage is one of the major factors behind the huge lucrative potential of the Forex market. There are many brokers offering up to 1000:1 trading leverage which allows the trader to make a huge amount of profit from a small investment. For instance, an account size of $100 with 1:100 leverage gives the trader access to the equivalent of $10K trading capital.

But having said all that, the abuse of high leverage will also lead to catastrophic losses if you are not a successful trader. It is a double edged sword, so be careful. That is why some jurisdictions like the USA limit their residents to a maximum of 50:1 leverage if using a US based broker. This is an attempt by the regulators to help prevent traders taking too big a position size that will damage their account significantly if things go wrong for them.

A smart trader would not be too concerned about what leverage is available to them as they would base their trade position size to fit within their defined money management rules. High leverage is only an issue for reckless or uneducated traders.

Bottom Line

Due to the technological advancement and exclusive features offered by brokers, Forex trading is now available to just about anyone that is over a certain age. They can experience high-speed trade execution associated with smart leverage to maximize their profits. But it is not as easy as it looks. It does require practice and a good understanding of how the markets work. On top of that, you have to have discipline and patience, and a sound trading plan. Once you have all of this under control, then you are well on your way to becoming a successful Forex trader.

Trading Parameters

Trading the Forex market and making a profit from it requires a sound knowledge about different trading parameters. Trading parameters are referred to as all the associated terms required to fully understand the Forex market.

Currency Pairs

The Forex market is traded in currency pairs. For Example "EUR/USD" and "GBP/USD" are two of the most popular traded currency pairs in the Forex market. The strength of one currency is always determined against another currency. . In the example of the EUR/USD, The EUR is known as the "base currency" and the USD is known as "quote currency." For instance, if the value of USD/JPY is 120.00, this means for 120 Japanese Yen you are going to get 1 USD.

Let's see some other examples:

AUD/USD = 0.7533
This means with 1 Australian Dollar you will get 0.7533 USD

GBP/USD = 1.4415
This means with 1 Great British Pound you will get 1.4415 USD

NZD/USD = .6839
This means with 1 New Zealand Dollar you will get 0.6839 USD

EUR/JPY = 121.39
This means with 1 Euro you will get 121.39 Japanese Yen

Bid and Ask

Forex traders are offered two choices in the quoted price when they trade any single pair - the bid price and the ask price. The bid price is the price that you need to pay in order to sell the pair in the Forex market whereas, the ask price refers to the buying price offered by the broker for the same pair.

'Ask price is always greater than the bid price regardless of the market situation'

Let's see some examples:

EUR/USD=1.1139/1.1142; If you wanted to buy this pair, you would buy it at 1.1142, and if you wanted to sell it, you would sell it at 1.1139

GBP/USD;=1.4420/1.4423; If you wanted to buy this pair, you would buy it at 1.4423, and if you wanted to sell it, you would sell it at1.4420

Pips and Pipettes

Pips are one of the smallest fractional movements that a currency pair can move. The amount of change in a currency pair is measured in pips. Generally, the pips are displayed in 4 decimal places. For example, if the value of EUR/USD is currently 1.1142, then for 3 pip advance in the market, the new value of EURUSD would be 1.1145.

You might be wondering what will be the next value of the EUR/USD for a 10 pip advance if its current value is 1.9999. If you are thinking about 2.0009, then you are absolutely correct. It just follows the simple addition and subtraction rules. The only difference being the JPY based pairs such as the USD/JPY, EUR/JPY, AUD/JPY etc, as these are normally displayed in 2 decimal places. An example would be the UDS/JPY quoted at 107.08.

These days many brokers offer fifth digit pricing for currency pairs which are known as "pipettes." To be precise 10 pipettes equals 1 pip. For example, the EURUSD price offered by fifth digit pricing broker is 1.11341. For the advance of 2 pipettes in the market, the new price will be 1.11343.

Trading with accounts that offer pipettes can be extremely beneficial since the trading can be done with greater precision. The same applies to the JPY pairs. If there are pipettes involved, then instead of only 2 decimal places, there will be 3 decimal places. Pipettes can be a little confusing at first as inexperienced traders forget that the 5th decimal place is not an actual full pip, but instead just 1/10th of a pip. This is simply something that the trader must be aware of.

Spread

The difference between the bid price and the ask price is known as the "spread".

Generally, all brokers use a variable spread which will vary from time to time depending on the volatility of the pair. If the average daily movement of a currency is higher, then we can expect a higher spread compared to less volatile times involving that particular currency. The spread is very important to the Forex trader as this is generally considered your cost of doing business.

Most brokers offer commission free trading, however they make their money by the spread the trader is forced to pay. For example, if the spread was 2 pips, then if the trader bought a currency pair and then immediately sold it before rice had a chance to move, then the trader would have lost 2 pips, as the trader buys at the ask price and sells at the bid price. This is where the broker makes up their commission.

Let's see some examples:

EUR/USD = 1.1139/1.1142
Here the spread is 0.0003 or 3 pips

GBP/USD = 1.4420/1.4424
Here the spread is 0.0004 or 4 pips

USD/JPY = 110.03/110.08
Here the spread is 0.05 or 5 pips
Lot size/ volume

Understanding the lot size/volume is very easy. But things get a little bit complicated when we go with unit calculations. However we won't go for the complex calculations. Every single pip that moves in our direction gives us profit. For instance, if we entered a long on the EURUSD at 1.1139 and the market moves 20 pips in our favor, and if we then close the trade, then the 20 pips is our profit.

Basically, lot size determines the pip value in the Forex market. The higher the lot size/volume, the bigger the pip value. A lot of Forex brokers refer to position size as 'volume'. It is not to be confused with overall volume traded as like in the Stock market, where they may say something like 'Apple was traded on lower volume today', which basically means there were less overall number of shares traded on Apple for that particular day. Volume in Forex generally refers to the position size.

For our better understanding, we have divided the Forex broker into three major groups:

- Standard lot broker
- Mini lot broker
- Micro lot broker

Standard lot broker	
1 standard lot	= $10/pip
0.1 standard lot	= $1/pip
0.01 standard lot	= $0.10/pip
10 standard lot	= $100/pip

Mini lot broker	
1 standard lot	= $1/pip
0.1 standard lot	= $0.10/pip
0.01 standard lot	= $0.01/pip
10 standard lot	= $10/pip

Micro lot broker	
1 standard lot	= $0.10/pip
0.1 standard lot	= $.01/pip
0.01 standard lot	= $0.001/pip
10 standard lot	= $1/pip

All of the above figures are based on USD based currency pairs ie EUR/USD, GBP/USD, AUD/USD etc.

On other pairs it is best to use a freely available Forex Pip Calculator as the calculation for lot size valuations can be a little confusing as it is a math formula based on the two individual currencies. Generally however, 1x standard lot on a Standard account can be considered to be approximately US$10.

Most other pairs are very close to this figure anyway, with possibly the EUR/GBP being the exception, which can be as high as US$15 per pip on a Standard lot.

Stop Loss and Take Profit

When you open a trade you can set your predefined stop loss and take profit levels.

So what is stop loss and take profit?

A stop loss is simply a predetermined price that you have decided on, that if your trade goes against you, then you no longer wish to be in that trade. If price hits your stop loss, then your trade is automatically closed by your broker and you accept the loss. A take profit is basically the opposite where you may have a good idea of where the market will run to according to your trading plan.

You can set a predetermined take profit and once price reaches that level, your trade is automatically closed by your broker and you accept that profit. You can always modify either of these levels as your trade progresses, but it is never really a good idea to move a stop loss further away from your original starting level. Things do change in the market, for example there may be major news coming out, where you want to tighten your stop loss up a little and extend your take profit etc. If you had entered a long on the GBPUSD at 1.1442 and put your stop loss 30 pips below the current market level, then no matter what, your trade would be closed automatically if the market reached the price of 1.1412.

Basically, a stop loss protects your account balance by minimizing the loss

On the contrary, when the trader places a 60 pips take profit on the same trade, then the market needs to reach the 1.1502 level for the trade to close and lock in that profit. There will be times where the trader may not get the exact price as nominated by them on either the stop loss or take profit due to various reasons, including very fast moving markets, or gapping in prices over the weekend etc. But generally, stop losses and take profit are normally filled very close to the selected price.

3

Forex Market Hours and Time Frames

The lucrative Forex market is open 24 hours a day and 5 days a week. There are many different kinds of traders like day traders, swing traders and scalpers. They all have their own preferred time frame and time zone. Initially, it might not sound so important but in the long run, this is one of the "key ingredients" of becoming a successful trader.

Professional traders have classified the market hours into three major sessions.

- The Asian session (major market: Tokyo)
  Opens at 7pm and closes at 4am (EST)

- The European session (major market: London)
  Opens at 3am and closes at 12pm (EST)

- The North American session (major market: New York)
  Opens at 8am and closes at 5pm (EST)

You might be wondering what the big deal is about these sessions? Don't worry! I will give you all the details about each one. But before going into the details, keep in mind it is important to consider a Forex trading session before taking a trade. Most of the struggling traders haven't considered this important fact in their trading career.

Professional traders trade specific pairs in specific sessions since they know they have a better chance of succeeding following this rule. If the "AUD/JPY" is traded in the US session then there is a low probability of success as there is very little economic activity for this particular pair in that session. On the contrary, if you chose to trade the "EUR/USD" during the US session you are sure to enjoy high volatility and profit making opportunities.

Asian Session

After the weekend, the Asian session brings the life back to the financial market by restoring the liquidity. In the Asian session, we can expect some possible movements in the JPY, AUD and NZD pairs since it's the time when the Asian and Pacific countries announce their major economic news. But if you trade other pairs like "EUR/USD and GBP/USD", then don't expect large movements or high volatility on these pairs.

European Session

The European session comes into action just before the closing of the Asian session. The European session is often referred to as the London session due to the fact that London is considered the financial capital of Europe. Traders usually trade the Euro, Pound and Swiss pairs in this session due to increased volatility.

North American Session

When the North American session kicks in, the Asian market has already closed and the European session is still open for a few more hours The US session has a large effect on any pairs involving the US and Canadian Dollars creating plenty of unique trading opportunities for the traders. Traders should be very careful during this session at times, as most of the major economic news is released due to the fact that the USD is considered the world's premier currency; therefore any news relating to the USD normally affects every other country.

Time Frames

So, what is a time frame?

Monitoring a certain pair for the defined period of time is known as the time frame. In general, all the trading platforms have various time frames as a built-in function. So if you were looking at a 1 hour candlestick chart, each candlestick represents 1 hour of time, showing the open, close and the range of what that particular pair did in that 1 hour. Same would apply to a 5 minute chart or a Monthly chart.

A Forex trader would choose a time frame that suits their trading style. For example, a long term trader my only refer to Daily charts whilst a day trader may use the 15 minute charts.

The most common time frames used by traders are:

- 1 minute
- 5 minute
- 15 minute
- 30 minute
- 1 hour
- 4 hour
- Daily
- Weekly
- Monthly

As mentioned above, with the help of time frame, we can identify four major parameters of price movement. If the trader uses the 4 hour time frame and elects to display either a candlestick chart or a bar chart, then the opening and closing price for the last four hours can be easily determined along with the high and low (range) during that 4 hour period.

Professional traders don't necessarily trade with a single time frame analysis. They may take their trading decisions based on multiple time frame analysis. So, what is multiple time frame analysis? It is the study of the price movement in different frequencies and different interval of time is known as multiple time frame analysis

Long term position traders or day traders prefer the higher time frame to trade the Forex market. They identify the prevailing trend in a currency pair from the monthly, weekly or the daily time frame analysis. For a more precise entry, they would then drop down to the 4-hour time frame. On the contrary, scalpers use shorter time frames like the 15 minute or the 30 minute charts to identify the prevailing trend in the market. After successful identification of the prevailing trend, they take their trade on the 1 minute or 5-minute charts.

Long Time Frame

It is believed that the better trading results are found by trading the longer time frames. However, this is not necessarily true for everyone, since it greatly depends on the trader's personality and trading skills. Long term position traders are generally more conservative traders and prefer wider stop loss looking for large market moves. Trading the longer time frames give more time to make decisions and also requires less time monitoring of the computer screen.

Short Time Frame

Short time frame traders are commonly known as "scalpers" or "day traders". As they are on the smaller time frames, they tend to use a tight stop loss and are looking for quick and small movements in the market. Their decision process has to be faster and they are normally glued to their screens during the duration of their preferred trading session.

Let's see an example of multiple time frame analysis on the following page:

USDCAD,weekly

Uptrend in weekly Chart

Figure (a): Uptrend on the weekly chart

Uptrend in daily Chart

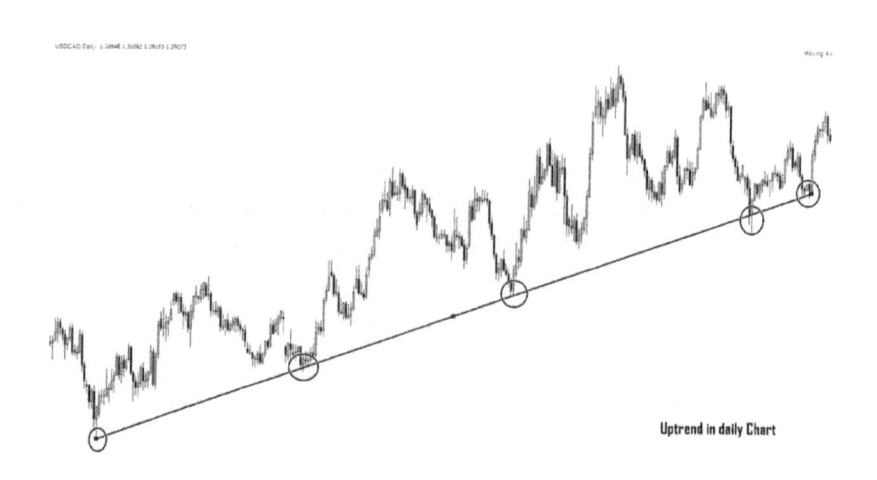

Figure (b): Uptrend on the daily chart

In the above figure (a), the trader first draws a valid trend line on the weekly chart. After successful identification of an uptrend on the weekly chart, the trader will look for confirmation on the daily chart. Surprisingly both the weekly and daily charts exhibit a clear uptrend on the USD/CAD pair. This type of analysis using different time frames is known as multiple time frame analysis. Multiple time frame analysis helps to filter out false or low probability trade signals in the Forex market. If there are dissimilarities with the trading signals on the different time frames, then the trader may consider ignoring those signals as they may prove to be false or low probability.

Best Time Frame to Trade

The forex market can be traded in the different sessions with different time frames. There is no best or worse time frame to trade. It is whatever is best suited to the individual trader as everyone circumstances are different. If you only had a few hours each day to trade, then you may choose to use the 30 minute and below charts, whereas a trader who can continuously monitor the markets, may decide on 1 hour and higher charts. The better, or smart way to take a trade, is by multiple time frame analysis, as it always a very good idea to know what the trend is, in at least one time frame higher or more. But at the end of the day, the trader has to be comfortable with the choice they make.

4

Three Major Types of Market Analysis

Trading any financial instrument can be very challenging for new traders. The next section will cover how to trade the Forex market with greater ease and a higher level of accuracy. Basically there are three major types of analysis with which to trade the Forex market successfully.

- Technical analysis

- Fundamental analysis

- Sentiment analysis

It's in human nature that people tend to choose the best one. In order to become a successful trader you must have a very good understanding of at least one these three types of analysis. The three types can complement each other where you can use a combination as you choose.

1. Technical Analysis

The study of the price movement of any pair regardless of any economic event is known as the technical analysis. In the Forex industry, there is a saying that "history tends to repeat itself".

Traders use the past price movement to determine the potential support and resistance levels of any pair to take their trade. They use different parameters and charts to identify the potential key reversal and entry points in the currency pair by using the technical analysis.

Let's look at an example of technical analysis:

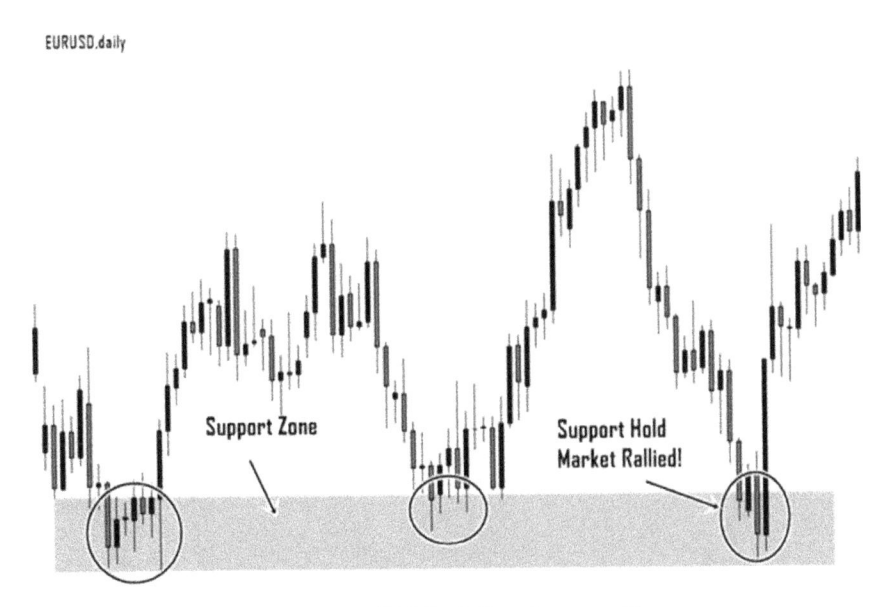

Figure: EUR/USD daily chart trading

In the above figure, the market tested the support zone twice. Support becomes much stronger when it is tested multiple times. At the third attempt, support held and price shot up for more than 800+ pips. Trading the Euro using this type of support zone is a classic example of technical analysis and trade execution.

Support and Resistance Levels

This is one of the most important parameters in technical analysis.

Traders use the support zone as the potential buying area, and look for selling opportunities at the resistance zone. Support and resistance in the

Forex market are drawn with a horizontal line on the chart. Some traders prefer to draw the support and resistance level with a single line, however professional traders consider support and resistance levels as a zone. A valid support and resistance line (or zone) will always have two connecting points with the straight line.

Trend Line

A well-known trading proverb is "The trend is your friend".

Professional traders use trend lines in order to assist with the identification of potential trades in the Forex market. A valid trend line will always have at least three connecting points on any currency pair. Trading using the trend line with price action signal confirmation and confluence can result in a higher probability of success for the trader.

Let's look at the technical analysis:

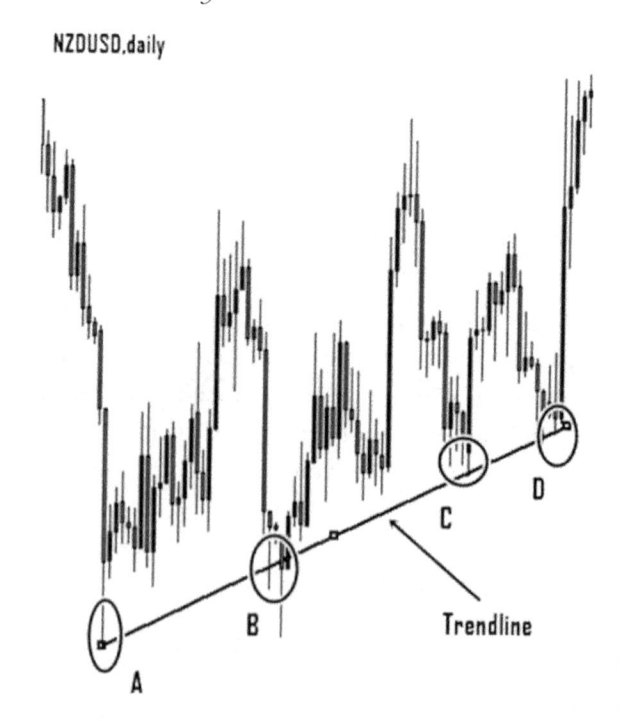

Figure: Trend line on the NZD/USD Daily chart, uptrend

In the previous figure, a valid trend line is drawn by connecting three major swing low points on the NZD/USD chart. A, B and C are the three major connecting points of the trend line. The trader will look for a buying opportunity at point D. Here the trend line acts as a sloping support level for the currency pair.

Price Action Analysis

The study of raw price data and candlestick formations is known as price action analysis. Candlestick confirmation at key support and resistance levels produce some very accurate trading signals. This is one of the most reliable and advanced technical analysis techniques that professional traders use to confirm trade entry. To be precise, price action traders are combining the fundamentals of technical analysis with the candlestick pattern to secure high probability trades in the Forex market.

If you would particularly like further information on Price Action, I have released another book on this topic, which provides an introduction to Price Action in Forex Trading.

Fibonacci Retracement Level and Technical Analysis

Fibonacci is one of the favorite tools used by many technical traders. Generally, long-term technical traders prefer using this tool as the longer time frames tend to comply with the levels created by the Fibonacci indicator, whereas the shorter time frames may not be as accurate. This strategy can be extremely profitable if executed properly.

Advantages of using Fibonacci retracement tools in the technical analysis:

- Helps to identify the current trend

- Recent Swing high and swing low can easily be identified

- Identifies key levels of the retracement (pullback) as noted below

It is one of the most widely used tools used in the technical analysis of any pair. The most significant retracement areas of this tool are the 38.2%, 50% and 61.8% levels. The Fibonacci retracement level should be drawn from the most recent "swing Low to swing High" for uptrend, and for down trend, "swing High to swing Low."

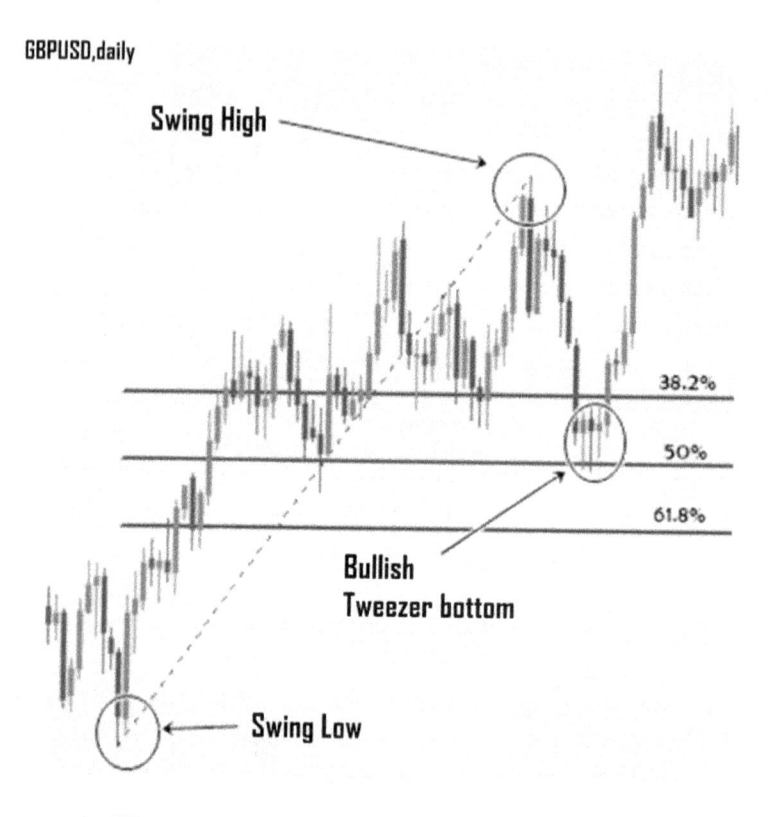

Figure: Fibonacci retracement level in an uptrend

Here the market formed a reliable tweezer bottom candlestick pattern on the 50 % level of the Fibonacci retracement. So it's a "buying opportunity" for the Fibonacci trader. Basically, the trader looks for a price action confirmation pattern at this important level to take the trade.

Trade Setup

Most of the Fibonacci traders prefer higher time frames to trade with

Fibonacci levels. In the prior example, Fibonacci retracement level was drawn from the most recent swing low to a relevant swing high. Traders then wait for the market to retrace back to the important Fibonacci levels. As we all know, markets do not generally travel in a straight line either up or down, as they tend to 'step' when in a trend. All Fibonacci is doing, is looking for those 'steps', where the main trend will resume.

Stop Loss and Take Profit

There are two ways to place a stop loss in Fibonacci trading. Those who are more concerned about their investment should put their stop loss just below the tweezer bottom or the decision-making candlestick pattern. Other traders may consider placing their stop loss just on the other side of the closest Fibonacci level from where they entered the trade. For example, if they were in a buy trade and took that buy trade off the 50% Fibonacci level, they may consider placing their stop loss just below the 61.8% Fibonacci level.

The potential profit of Fibonacci trading is extremely high. Look for a risk reward ratio of at least 1:3 when you trade these important levels. It is generally a good idea to book half of your profit when it shows momentum in the trend, where you could also consider moving to stop loss to break even so as it then becomes a 'no risk' trade that has already made a small profit. Generally if price then breaks the high or the low that formed the Fibonacci levels, then this is a very good sign that the trend is continuing which should result in a very good profit.

Chart Patterns

There are many different kinds of chart patterns that traders use in their technical analysis arsenal. Chart pattern trading has a higher chance of success when it is looked at in conjunction with price action confirmation.

The 'double bottom' chart pattern is a bullish reversal chart pattern. This chart pattern indicates that the prevailing bearish trend is losing momentum and a new uptrend is going to rule the market. This type of pattern is usually formed after a long decisive move in the market. Professional traders use this chart pattern to ride the new bullish trend from the very beginning of the reversal. Since trading the 'double bottom' pattern is a counter trend technique, price action confirmation is also required to help confirm that price is indeed reversing to the opposite direction.

Let's look at an example of a 'double bottom' chart pattern:

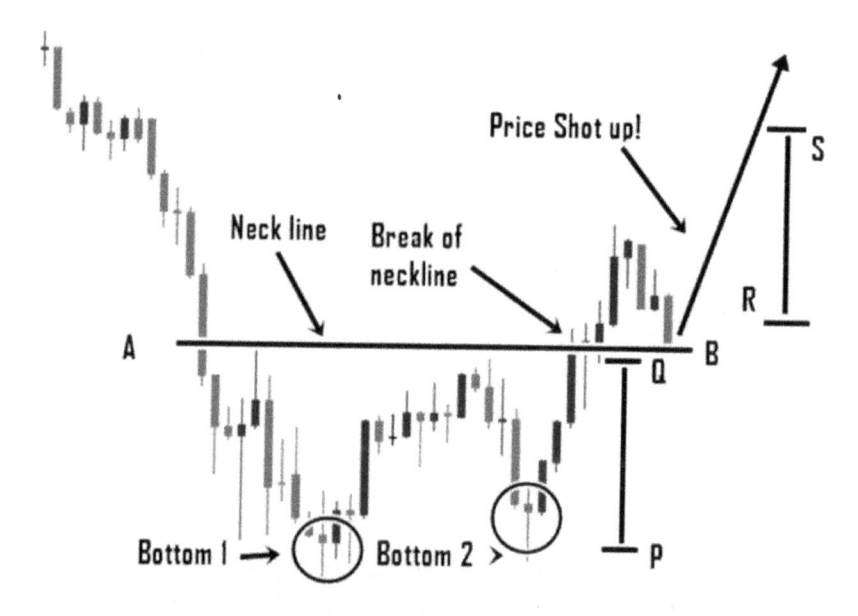

Figure: Double bottom chart pattern

In the above figure, "Bottom 1 and Bottom 2" are formed near the same level. It's important that the low of Bottom 2 doesn't go beyond the Bottom 1 low. The neckline acts as a temporary resistance level for price. The bullish pin bar at the Bottom 2 level confirms that price has bottomed down and is ready to head up. The double bottom pattern is said to be confirmed and validated when price then breaks the neckline.

Technical Setup

Trading the 'double bottom' or 'double top' pattern is relatively easy if price action confirmation is used to confirm the trade entry. The trader waits for the formation of Bottom 1 and of Bottom 2. The bullish pin bar then confirms the validation of Bottom 2. Aggressive traders can immediately take a buy entry from that bullish confirmation candlestick pattern. Stop loss should be placed just below the low of the confirmation candlestick pattern.

More conservative traders may choose to wait for a valid breakout of the neckline region before taking their trade. Price may even retrace back to the neckline area, before eventually heading up. If you missed the trade entry on the first break, this may present another opportunity for an entry. When price does take of in the preferred direction, then placement of the stop loss just below the neckline would be a good place for it.

There are numerous ways of using technical analysis in the Forex market. Indicators, moving averages, chart patterns etc, are all the tools that traders use to assist them with their technical analysis of the Forex market. But currency trading using technical analysis only is generally not good enough. Traders need to be aware of the fundamentals also. This is normally the news that moves the market. You don't necessarily have to completely understand it, but at least be aware of it and have a basic understanding of it. The next section will cover fundamental analysis and how it affects the market. Technical analysis combined with fundamental analysis provides much more reliable and accurate trading signals.

2. Fundamental Analysis

Fundamental analysis is the study of the economic news release data. It helps the trader to get an overall picture of a country's economic strength. With the help of fundamental analysis, long-term trend change and short-term trend change in most currency pairs can easily be identified. Traders use major economic news release data to determine if there is any potential trend reversal presenting in the market.

The interest rate decision of any country plays an important role in the economy of that country. If the interest rate is increased, then this generally means that the country's economy is performing well. There is the direct reflection of the interest rate hike in the Forex market. For instance, if we see that the USD/CHF is in a downtrend for two weeks, but the Federal Reserve Bank holds a meeting and decides to hike their interest rate, which could result in a major change in the trend of this USD pair. The downtrend in USD/CHF will end with a possibility of a new uptrend beginning.

> ## 'Traders should be very cautious when trading around the news'

The unemployment figures also play a vital role in the Forex market, as do speeches by important members of the various banks and financial institutions that dictate market conditions. The majority of news releases are set at predetermined times so that traders can be ready for that particular release. It is normal to see what the particular figure or statement was at the last release and also what is expected this time around. Now if this figure falls within expectations, then normally there is very little market movement after the event as it was already built into price prior to the release. It is when the expectations are widely wrong on either side that will cause violent reactions in price movement.

3. Sentiment Analysis

This is the last thing that traders need to know to complete their trading arsenal. Trading with market sentiment requires time and practice, and it's something that we can't learn by reading books or watching videos. It is a gradual skill the trader develops just by watching markets and actually trading them, and also considering all the available information regarding a particular currency whether that be from news channels or social media etc. Consider it something like a 'gut feel' or 'gut instinct'. Every trader trades the market in their own way and even though their technical and fundamental analysis could be exactly the same, it will be the sentiment analysis that makes the difference between a winning trader and a losing trader.

Just to summarize this section, a successful trader will use a combination of technical analysis and fundamental analysis to trade the Forex market. Now this will vary from trader to trader, whereas some traders will rely on one aspect more heavily than the other. But the one thing all that all good traders do share and that is a good understanding of sentiment analysis. In other words, they will recognize a good (or bad) set up when they see it and will (or will not) take the trade based on that final bit of analysis. It is just a skill that comes with many years of practice where an outsider might consider that trader to have a sixth sense so to speak. But the good news is that all traders can learn these skills over time.

5

Choosing the Right Broker

There are many Forex brokers across the world and choosing the right one for you can be a challenge. It's important that you feel comfortable with your trading platform and broker's service. There are number of things you should consider before choosing a broker.

> 'There are many brokers who claim to offer excellent services in terms of trading, but be sure that your broker is regulated by the relevant authorities within their jurisdiction'

Reliability and Security

Generally countries like the USA, the UK, Australia, Canada, New Zealand etc. all have fairly strict rules and regulations in place that not only protect the trader, but also ensure that the broker complies with all their necessary rules and regulations. This is to ensure a level playing field for all parties involved, and also to offer some sort of protection to both the trader and the broker. These rules may seem onerous to some, but they are there for a reason and you would be well advised to use a broker that does comply.

There are countries where brokers are based, where there are not a strict protection type rules in place. I'm certainly not suggesting all broker in these jurisdictions are dishonest, but why would the trader risk it when there are plenty of other options available? A trader may be even more comfortable with using a broker within their home country, which is a valid point also, but in any case all traders must conduct extensive due diligence when choosing a broker. Peace of mind is an important issue!

Initial Trading Capital

As there is such a low cost entry price to open a Forex trading account, some brokers offer minimum account deposits of $50 to $200. These same brokers may offer outrageous leverage of sometimes up to 1000:1. They may also offer sign up bonuses or other incentives to go with them. Generally these are the brokers to stay clear of as they are normally based in jurisdictions that may be a little 'loose' with their rules and regulations. Again, this is not suggesting that all brokers that offer these types of deals are dishonest, but these can be seen as red flags regarding a broker that may not offer the customer service you would expect, nor still be around in a few years' time.

If you can only afford to open a small account initially, then I would suggest that you test the waters with these types of brokers and see if you can withdraw your profits without any problem. This way you leave the minimum amount for funds under their control, and in the meantime you could be building your bank account to go with a more reputable broker at a future date.

Spreads

This is an important issue when choosing a broker. There are some brokers that offer excellent spreads compared to others. But offering an excellent spread is not necessarily always the best option. You should also consider how well your trades are executed and whether it's a fixed spread broker or variable spread broker.

Typically top end brokers offer less than a 2 pip spread on the most commonly traded pair, the EUR/USD. So if your selected broker is charging more than this spread on the EUR/USD during normal market conditions, then you should reconsider your choice of broker.

The spread is crucial for the scalper and news traders. Even though it might seem to be unimportant for the long term traders but it is something they should also consider. As market conditions change due to volatility created by major news etc, then expect spreads to vary at times also to match this volatility. A pair may be trading at 1.5 pip spread during normal trading activity, but could blow out to a spread of between 8 and 10 pips during a volatile period. This could be just for a few seconds or minutes, where once the markets settle, then the normal spread is resumed. Most decent brokers will trade like this, but a broker that may not be as reputable, may hold their spreads at a constant price throughout the volatile period. Do not use a broker that does this as something is just not right.

Deposits and Withdrawals

This is one of the key factors that the traders should consider before choosing their broker.

A good broker should have different payment gateways for quick deposits and withdrawals. It's true that some withdrawal procedures may take 1-3 business days with top class brokers but make sure that your broker doesn't exceed the time period stated in their withdrawal section. Their website should contain clear and concise information regarding deposit and withdrawal conditions do there is no misunderstanding.

Trading Platform

This is crucial for all the traders who want to trade the financial markets.

Make sure that your broker offers the right trading platform which is compatible with your trading style. For example, you may trade off the 10 minute charts, but if your broker doesn't offer 10 minute charts, why would you go with them? Also some brokers will not permit high frequency trading, so it is something the trader would have to consider if that was their style of trading. Trade execution should be extremely fast with little or no slippage. It's true that sometimes you will face slippage with top class brokers but there is no avoiding that in fast moving markets. Generally due to the high liquidity of the Forex market, the majority of trade orders are filled at the nominated price.

Customer Service

There are times that you may experience some technical difficulties while dealing with a broker. So make sure that the customer service representatives are well aware of handling such situations. Most of the better brokers will allocate an Account Manager to each trader, so it can be beneficial to chat with the company representative at various times to get a feel for their skills and availability. Remember, a good broker will always have experienced and knowledgeable customer service representatives which should be easily contactable either by phone, live chat or email. If you can't get a hold of anyone at your broker's office, it is time to withdraw your funds and find a new broker as soon as possible.

Account Types

There are many different types of accounts offered by Forex brokers, as there are a few different variations of platform types. The actual account types vary from broker to broker but it is normally based on the trader's initial account deposit.

So for example, if you were depositing $50,000 into an account, the broker may offer you a Standard account with a maximum leverage of 200:1, whereas a trader depositing $500 may be offered a Mini account with leverage of 400:1 The different trading platforms on offer may suit different traders with different makes of computers, or those after web based platforms instead of downloadable software etc.

In conclusion, if the you are a trader and having difficulty in choosing a broker, there are reputable companies around like Forest Park FX that will help the trader decide which broker will best suits the trader's needs taking their particular circumstances into account. A company like Forest park FX have already done the necessary due diligence on the brokers on their list, and can therefore just match them to their clients. This service does not cost the trader anything as the broker pays Forest Park FX a small percentage of the spread for every trade the trader takes. There is also the possibility of the actual trader receiving a rebate from the company as an extra bonus. It is certainly worth having a chat with them or another similar type company if you can't decide on a broker.

Note: I have no affiliation with Forest Park FX other than being a satisfied customer.

One Final Note on Brokers

It is strongly suggested that you do not put all of your available trading funds with one broker. Even though you may have chosen a very well-known broker from an excellent jurisdiction when it comes to rules and regulations, there is always the possibility that something could go wrong. A perfect recent example of this was back in January 2015, Alpari UK was caught out by the Swiss de-pegging their currency from the Euro. Alpari UK was a well-known and very respected broker that went to the wall because of this. The good news was that most clients' funds were eventually returned due to the UK's very good protection laws, however it took some months for this process to play out. So it can happen to any broker. A way around this is to split your funds between two or more reputable brokers, or even keep funds in a reserve bank account that be can be easily transferred to your brokerage account if required, but trade size as if those funds were in your brokerage account. It is certainly better to be safe than sorry.

6

The Truth About Successful Forex Trading

There has always been a mystery about the Forex market. Many have searched for the Holy Grail at a certain period in their trading career. So, is there a holy grail in trading forex? It seems to be the million dollar question, but the answer is pretty simple!

'There is NO Holy Grail In Forex Trading'

People are so fascinated with online Forex trading due to its lucrative opportunity and potential financial freedom and the fact that Forex trading has never been as easy as it is now. Yet the number of successful traders is very low when it comes to long term successful trading. Recent data by a leading Forex Broker showed that the majority of traders were actually right in their analysis of market direction, but it was other factors that let them down, such as poor trade management eg. Taking bigger losses than profits.

So are there any consistently successful Forex traders? The simple answer is YES. There are many successful traders out there who are comfortably making profits. They have quit their day job and have taken Forex trading on as a full-time profession. However, many new to the scene have also jumped straight into the Forex market with their hard earned cash and ended up quickly losing everything. There is a saying about the successful trader that you might like to consider that You will never see a successful trader with an easy past. All of them have gone through an extensive learning curve and self-development before hitting success.

It requires the combination of three skills to become successful in Forex Trading:

1. You must have a good knowledge of technical analysis, fundamental analysis and the correct mindset. It's human nature that poor traders can't accept losses whereas a good trader accepts that losses are just a part of the process, learning from them and then moving onto the next trade. Consider your loss as the capital cost of learning the Forex market.

2. Patience has its own reward. Forex trading requires a great deal of perseverance. New traders repeatedly fail to stick with their trading rules resulting in them jumping into a trade without any rational logic. They let their emotions take control of themselves. If you want to be a successful trader then you must know how to manage your emotions efficiently.

   Don't get overwhelmed with a couple of big winning trades and don't get disheartened by a series of losing trades. Even the most successful traders in today's world will have losing months. However, they are committed to their long-term goals and trade with strict discipline, following their rules through both good and bad times. Trade what you see not what you believe.

3. Every businessman always has realistic expectations from their investment. Forex trading is also considered to be one of the smart businesses in the world, but in reality, some people think that it's a get rich quick scheme. They hope for an unrealistic profit from a small investment. It's true that sometimes they will get lucky, resulting in big winnings due to the high leverage provided by the broker, but in the long run they are sure to blow up their account. Statistical data shows however, that 90-95% of new traders fail within

a few months of opening an account.

On the contrary, professional traders manage their trading very efficiently and can earn a return of 5-10% per month. How do they do it? They simply follow the golden rules of trading, which is a sound trading method, discipline and very good money management rules.

The two simple rules for success:

Rule #1
Stick to your trading plan and be disciplined, regardless of the situation

Rule #2
Always follow Rule # 1

The Secret of Success

In order to become a successful Forex trader there are six key elements and characteristics that every trader should possess:

1. *Realistic expectations*

   Most traders live in a dream world and have unrealistic expectations, looking to make huge profits quickly. Trading the financial market is not about a week, or a month, rather it's a consistent overall return over months, or even years that matter. Take your time, read more and continue to learn.

2. *Trade with adequate capital*

   Forex trading can be a bumpy ride and you will have some losing months. Make sure you have enough capital to support your losing months so that you can continue to trade. Consider this; if you have a goal to earn $2,000 a month, then you would require an initial trading account balance of something much greater than this. For example, starting with a $500 trading account would not produce that sort of return. It may eventually, with the power of compounding over time, but not from day one. So have enough capital to meet your goals and also cover the losing periods.

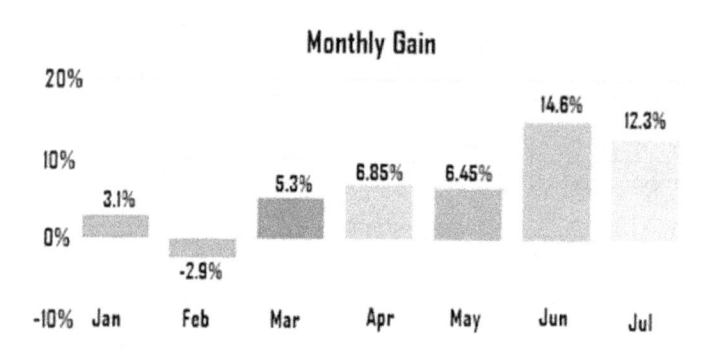

Monthly Gain

Month	Gain
Jan	3.1%
Feb	-2.9%
Mar	5.3%
Apr	6.85%
May	6.45%
Jun	14.6%
Jul	12.3%

Figure: 7 Month gain with one losing month

3. *An understanding of technical and fundamental analysis*

As a trader you must have a good understanding of technical analysis and/or fundament analysis. Clear knowledge about both technical and fundamental analysis is an important factor. Not all successful traders use both, but those that don't at least have a very good understanding and awareness of the other.

4. *Suitable trading strategy/plan*

You must develop a simple and consistent trading strategy that fits your personality and circumstances.. In a word, choose a trading strategy that is comfortable for you.

5. *Money management*

Your trading strategy should include valid entry and exit rules. But these are worthless if you don't have a sound money management plan. This plan dictates trade size for each trade, which in turn will control losing streaks ensuring you have enough capital to continue trading. When the winning streak presents, then because of your money management, you will be in a position to take full advantage of it.

6. *Correct mindset*

Any type of trading is tough on the mind, and Forex trading is no different. You will experience a continuous rollercoaster of emotions at times. It is the human mind that is the hardest hurdle to overcome when trading. You tend to see things a lot differently when real money is on the line. For example, traders tend to let their losses run out of control and cut their profits of quickly, whereas it should be the exact opposite. Easier said than done, I know. Having a disciplined mind does come with practice and time, where you just have to have faith in your trading plan and follow it to the letter, whether that be through the good times or the bad times. Discipline I've already mentioned, but a successful trader also requires patience and then the courage to act.

To summarize: where a trader has realistic goals, adequate capital, understands the markets, has a decent trading system, implements sound money management and can keep their emotions in check then, there is no reason why that person shouldn't become a successful Forex trader.

7

Two Simple Robust Trading Strategies

In the following section you will see two simple trading strategies examples.

1. Trading the USD/CHF daily chart

The USD/CHF, often referred to as the "Swissy" is one of the most popular traded pairs. It is often considered as the safe investment due to the strength and nonpartisan character of Switzerland's economy. It is traditionally a pair that trends very well on the Daily chart and therefore is an excellent vehicle for this example strategy.

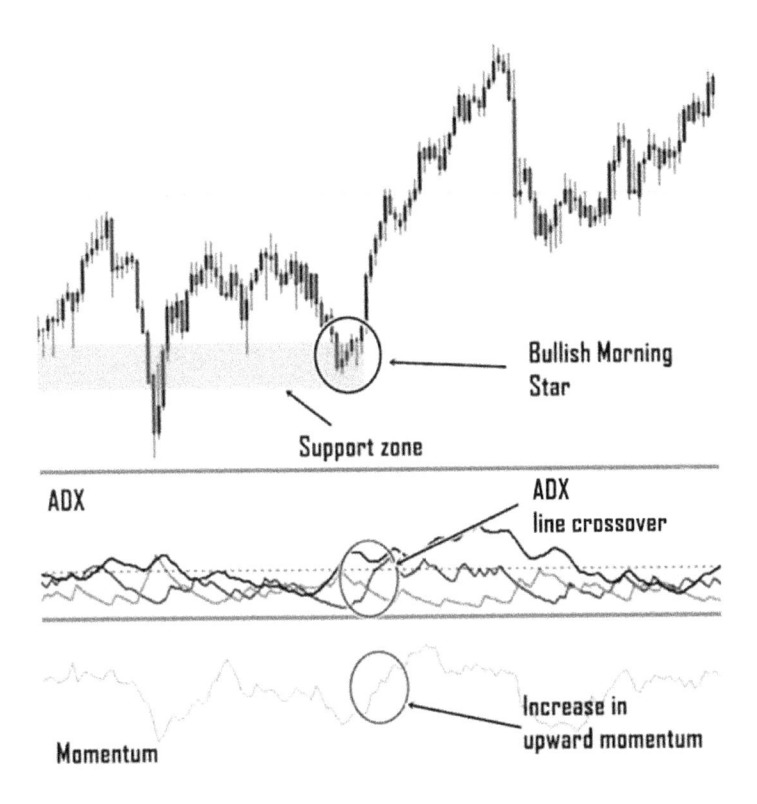

Figure: USD/CHF daily chart trading strategy with the ADX and Momentum indicators

- In the above figure, the price formed a bullish morning star pattern right at the support zone.

- The trader then waits for the ADX indicator confirmation.

- Last but not the least; the trade is only executed with the rising momentum of the pair.

- Both the ADX and Momentum indicators are simple technical indicators that are freely available on most trading platforms.

Trading condition and entry signal

This trading strategy is based on trading with the current trend. Although it can also act as a reversal pattern for the USD/CHF on the Daily chart, however the best result is found when traded in the direction of the major trend.

- The Trader identifies the potential support and resistance zone of the pair for taking high probability trades.

- The support or the resistance zone should be tested at least twice.

- After successful identification of the support and resistance level, the Trader then looks for a price action confirmation signal at the support zone for uptrend and at the resistance zone for the downtrend. This is generally achieved by recognizing candlestick patterns. Candlestick patterns are covered in the Price Action Book and the link has been included in Part 3.

- The Trader then looks for a crossover on the ADX indicator for confirmation on taking their trade. When the green line is above red line it indicates a possible uptrend scenario and when the green line is below the red line, it indicates a possible downtrend.

- With regards to the Momentum indicator, there should be clear indication of rising momentum before taking the trade. Without a clear indication of momentum, the trade should not be taken.

- The stop loss should be set just below the support level for a bullish trend (buy trade) and for a bearish trend (sell trade), it is set just above the key resistance level.

- A trader could use a trailing stop loss to maximize their profit potential while trading with this strategy.

2. Trading the USD/CAD Daily chart

USD/CAD is another one of the most trending pairs in the Forex market. Both long term traders and day traders love to trade this pair because of the long prevailing trends. A simple strategy has now been developed trading this pair by using only two Exponential Moving Averages and the ATR (Average True Range) indicator. Again, indicators are freely available on most trading platforms.

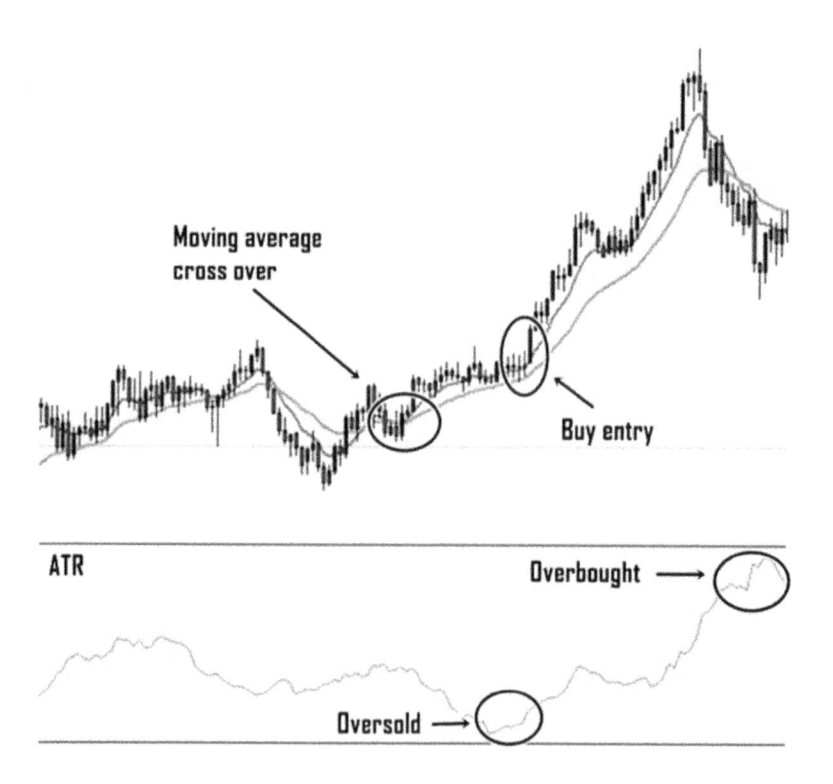

Figure: USD/CAD daily chart with 21 days and 8 day exponential moving average

.In the above figure, two exponential Moving Averages and the ATR indicator are used to trade this trending pair. The trader simply uses a Moving

Average crossover and previous support and resistance zone for identifying the potential entry point. The ATR indicator serves as the filter to take the best possible trade.

Trading condition and entry signal

Two Exponential Moving Averages should be used while trading this strategy. That being the 8 and 21.

- The Trader waits patiently for the Moving Average crossover to identify their potential trade setup. When the 8-day Exponential Moving Average is above the 21-day Exponential Moving Average, the trader looks for buying opportunities. Bearish opportunities are presented on the chart when the 8 day EMA is below the 21 day EMA.

- Once the crossover of the Moving Averages has been confirmed, the trader will look for previous support and resistance level to enter into the trade.

- The ATR indicator should be in the overbought condition for a sell setup, and for the buy setup it, should be in an oversold condition.

- Once the trade is executed, the trader should set their stop loss below or above the previous support or resistance level depending on the direction of the trade.

- As long as the two EMAs don't cross back again, the trader can ride the trade with confidence by trailing their stop loss at a safe distance behind price

- The trader takes their profit when the EMAs cross again, which may result in a trade in the opposite direction.

8

Conclusion and EA Offer

Well, this brings us to the end of the book.

Now you have been introduced to the basics of currency trading, you have the foundations to take this further if it has caught your interest. There is an abundance of information out there and it will be beneficial for you to tap into recommended resources on the following page:

Would you be interested in receiving the Trading Robot associated with my other book *Forex: A Powerful MT4 Trading Robot to Maximize Profits?* The International Amazon Link is provided below if you would like further details (case sensitive):

http://lrd.to/Forex-Trading-Robot

To find out how you can download the SMSF Trading Robot, designed for the MT4 platform, simply go to the following (case sensitive) and you will be provided with finer details:

http://eepurl.com/b7XjD1

* Please remember, if you use AOL, Yahoo, Gmail or Hotmail, these

providers deliver mail in small batches which can sometimes result in emails taking up to 24 hours to come through. Also, please check your spam/junk folders, if nothing comes through. Failing all the above, if it doesn't arrive, drop me a line at:

MM.ForexRobots@gmail.com

You can rest assured that unlike many others, I am not into upselling, side selling, sharing your details or spamming you! I don't have time, nor am I interested in doing so. I may share some valuable information with you occasionally, but this is only likely to be a few times a year.

9

Recommended Resources

Reading

Forex – The Basics Explained in Simple Terms
Jim Brown

MT4 High Probability Forex Trading Method
Jim Brown

An Introduction to Forex Trading - Forex Trading Using Price Action
Michelle Michaels

Forex: A Powerful MT4 Trading Robot to Maximize Profits
Michelle Michaels

High probability trading: take the steps to become a successful trader 1st Edition
Marcel Link

The Little Book of Market Wizards: Lessons from the Greatest Traders
Jack D. Schwager

Adventures of a Currency Trader: A Fable about Trading, Courage, and Doing the Right - Thing (Wiley Trading)
Rob Booker

Inventory Trading: How I Run My Trading Account Like a Retail Inventory Manager
Shonn Campbell

Trading in the Zone: Master the Market with Confidence, Discipline and a Winning
Mark Douglas

Forums

- Forex Factory
- Forex TSD
- Steve Hopwood
- Babypips
- Donna Forex

Podcasts

- 52 Traders
- Chat With Traders
- Desire to Trade
- The Booker Report
- The Traders Podcast
- Trader Radio
- Trend Following
- Truth About FX

Facebook Page

While I don't bother with Facebook myself, the following page is owned by personal friend, Jim Brown, who trades fulltime. On this newly created page he shares a great deal of Forex related information with his followers—

feel free to check it out. He is very welcoming and an all-round good Forex guy to connect with. The following link is case sensitive:

http://bit.ly/JAGfx

ABOUT THE AUTHOR

Michelle Michaels has had an interest in trading the financial markets dating back to the late 90's, when she first tried her hand at Futures trading. This was followed by Stock and Options trading and she eventually settled on concentrating all of her efforts into Forex trading in 2004. This has been her passion since, and she has had some great success along the way.

Michelle eventually realized that her trading style could be used across all financial markets. Primarily a Swing Trader, trading from the 4hr and Daily charts, Michelle also has a strong interest in different trading methods and converting those methods into trading robots (algorithmic trading) on the popular Metatrader (MT4) platform. As Michelle is now settled on her trading methods and enjoying the profits from it, in her quiet time she shares her knowledge with other traders and those new to the trading world regarding what she has learned along the way.

CPSIA information can be obtained
at www.ICGtesting.com
Printed in the USA
LVHW031810180820
663388LV00003B/340